U.S. Department of Justice
Office of Justice Programs
National Institute of Justice

I0448767

NIJ

2005   2006   2007   2008   2009   **2010**   2011

NIJ ANNUAL REPORT

U.S. Department of Justice
Office of Justice Programs
810 Seventh St. N.W.
Washington DC, 20531

Eric H. Holder Jr.
Attorney General

Laurie O. Robinson
Assistant Attorney General

John H. Laub
Director, National Institute of Justice

This and other publications and products of
the National Institute of Justice can be
found at:

National Institute of Justice
http://www.nij.gov

Office of Justice Programs
Innovation • Partnerships • Safer
Neighborhoods
http://www.ojp.usdoj.gov

To the President, the Attorney General and the Congress:

It is my honor to transmit the National Institute of Justice's annual report on research, development and evaluation for fiscal year 2010, pursuant to Title I of the Omnibus Crime Control and Safe Streets Act of 1968 and Title II of the Homeland Security Act of 2002.

Respectfully submitted,

John H. Laub,
Director, National Institute of Justice

INTRODUCTION

The National Institute of Justice is the only federal agency devoted solely to bringing the benefits of scientific research and technology development to the nation's criminal justice system.

NIJ is the research, development and evaluation arm of the U.S. Department of Justice. It helps criminal justice professionals perform better on the job by conducting basic and applied research, assessing new technologies, promoting innovations and evaluating programs to learn what works and what does not work.

NIJ applies a rigorous scientific approach to its endeavors. Researchers harness the power of science to make the American justice system more effective, more efficient and more equitable. Projects range from measuring the extent and nature of emerging crimes to using innovative DNA analysis to identify violent criminals. The Institute works closely with criminal justice professionals and researchers to help inform its research agenda.

STRATEGIC CHALLENGES 2010
REDUCING CRIME AND PROMOTING
JUSTICE

The National Institute of Justice is committed to becoming a transformative force in the criminal justice field by meeting five strategic challenges:

1. **FOSTERING SCIENCE-BASED CRIMINAL JUSTICE PRACTICE**: Supporting rigorous scientific research to ensure the safety of families, schools and communities.

2. **TRANSLATING KNOWLEDGE TO PRACTICE**: Disseminating rigorous scientific research to criminal justice professionals to advance what works best in crime prevention and reduction.

3. **ADVANCING TECHNOLOGY**: Building a more efficient, effective and fair criminal justice system.

4. **WORKING ACROSS DISCIPLINES**: Drawing on physical, forensic and social sciences to reduce crime and promote justice.

5. **ADOPTING A GLOBAL PERSPECTIVE**: Understanding crime rates and their social context at home and abroad.

NEW DIRECTOR JOINS NIJ

John H. Laub, Ph.D., was nominated by President Barack Obama to be the NIJ director. Laub was confirmed by the U.S. Senate in June 2010. He officially joined NIJ in July 2010. Before coming to NIJ, Laub was a Distinguished University Professor in the Department of Criminology and Criminal Justice at the University of Maryland. He also served as a Visiting Scholar at Harvard University's Institute for Quantitative Social Science. Laub is best known as the co-author of two award-winning books from Harvard University Press: *Crime in the Making: Pathways and Turning Points Through Life* (1993) and *Shared Beginnings, Divergent Lives: Delinquent Boys to Age 70* (2003). Both Laub and his longtime collaborator, Robert Sampson of Harvard University, have been named as the joint recipients of the 2011 Stockholm Prize in Criminology for their research showing how and why criminals stop offending.

EVALUATION OF THE NATIONAL INSTITUTE OF JUSTICE

NIJ requested and funded an evaluation by The National Academy of Sciences that examined the full range of the Institute's programs and priorities in an effort to determine the agency's capacity for meeting the needs of the criminal justice field. The report, *Strengthening the National Institute of Justice,* was released in July 2010. NIJ's director and staff are using the report as a springboard to make transformative changes at the Institute.

HIGHLIGHTS OF THE YEAR

The following pages provide just a sampling of the most prominent work undertaken by NIJ.

TABLE OF CONTENTS

CHAPTER 1:

FOSTERING SCIENCE-BASED CRIMINAL JUSTICE PRACTICE

Civil Protective Orders

A recent study looked at the impact of domestic violence victims getting civil protective orders in five Kentucky jurisdictions. It found the orders make a difference in safety, fear levels and cost savings. However, urban and rural populations reported significant differences. Civil protective orders, sometimes known as restraining orders, may include ordering an assailant to avoid a victim's home and workplace. They may also forbid any contact with the victim, including by mail or telephone. Half the women who got a protective order did not experience a violation within the following six months. Of the half who experienced violations in that time, the levels of violence and abuse declined significantly compared to the six months before the court issued a protective order.

Urban and rural women had similar views of how effective the protective orders were. However, rural women experienced more barriers to getting an order and having that order enforced, thus providing them less relief from fear and abuse. The study further explored the role of stalking in protective order violations and quantified the overall cost to society.

This research showed the value of protective orders in domestic violence cases.

> ➢ Read "Perspectives on Civil Protection Orders in Domestic Violence Cases: The Rural and Urban Divide" by Nikki Hawkins in NIJ Journal no. 266 at http://www.nij.gov/journals/266/perspectives.htm.

Use of Force

A study of less lethal technologies found that law enforcement use of Tasers and pepper spray can reduce injuries to officers and suspects alike. During the last two decades, new technologies have emerged that offer the promise of more effective control for police officers over uncooperative suspects with fewer risks of injuries to either party. Pepper spray was among the first of these less lethal weapons to achieve widespread adoption by police forces. Tasers and other conducted energy devices (CEDs) have grown in popularity in recent years. Taser use has become increasingly common in the line of duty, with industry estimates indicating that more than 11,500 law enforcement agencies nationwide use them. Further, most agencies allow use of Tasers by their rank-and-file in an array of arrest situations.

The study found that during arrests, the use of physical force and hands-on control in attempts to subdue a resistant or fleeing suspect increases the odds of injury to law enforcement officers by more than 300 percent. For suspects, the odds rose by more than 50 percent. Conversely, the use of pepper spray was shown to reduce the rate of suspect injury by up to 70 percent, while Taser use led to a decrease in injuries in both suspects and law enforcement by up to 60 percent. Among the agencies included in the study, Tasers were used four to five times more often than pepper spray. Use of these weapons, however, is not without risk (sometimes, Tasers and pepper spray have been associated with in-custody deaths), and proper training and policies are critical to a department's successful use of these tools.

➤ See "Multi-Method Evaluation of Police Use of Force Outcomes" by Geoffrey P. Alpert et al. at http://www.ncjrs.gov/pdffiles1/nij/grants/231176.pdf.

Evaluation of Automatic License Plate Reader Technology

NIJ is funding a Police Executive Research Forum study, the first large-scale randomized experiment of the effectiveness of technology that can automatically read license plates using cameras and computer systems. Law enforcement officials believe the technology may be useful in quickly solving auto theft cases and may have applications to a wide variety of other crimes as well. The study is being conducted with the Mesa Police Department in Arizona. Researchers have collected baseline data on the hot spots, transit routes, and destination points for auto theft in Mesa. They also conducted mapping analyses to identify the highest rate hot routes for auto theft in Mesa. Then they combined that information with detective and patrol officer suggested routes (for those places that do not show up in the crime statistics). The research team is working with a lead detective to oversee the experiment. Early results showed the readers were effective at identifying stolen cars. Arrests for car theft also increased. The final results are due in 2011.

Evaluation of School-based Anti-bullying Programs

NIJ sponsored an evaluation of existing anti-bullying programs in America and several European countries to learn which programs work and what contributes to their success.

The most important program elements associated with a decrease in both bullying and victimization were parent training and meetings, disciplinary methods, the duration of the program for children and teachers and the intensity of the program for children and teachers.

The most important program elements associated with a decrease in bullying (but not victimization) were:

- parent training and meetings
- Improved playground supervision
- disciplinary methods
- classroom management
- teacher training
- classroom rules
- whole school anti-bullying policies
- school conferences
- information for parents
- cooperative work groups

School conferences involved school assemblies that told children about bullying. In many programs, these conferences were organized after the pre-test data collection and aimed to tell students about the extent of bullying behavior in their school. This was seen as a first way to sensitize students to bullying and as a means of announcing the formal beginning of the intervention program in the school.

Cooperative work group refers to the cooperation among different professionals (usually among teachers and some other professional groups) in working with bullies and victims of bullying. Classroom management included techniques to detect and deal with bullying. Improved playground supervision aimed to identify "hot-spots" or "hot-times" of bullying, mostly during playtime or lunch time, and provided better supervision of children.

> See "School-Based Programs to Reduce Bullying and Victimization" by David P. Farrington and Maria M. Ttofi at http://www.ncjrs.gov/pdffiles1/nij/grants/229377.pdf.

Reentry

NIJ-sponsored research showing some of the difficulties offenders have in finding employment after their release from prison or jail. Using an experimental audit research design, matched pairs of individuals applied for real entry-level jobs to test the degree to which a criminal record affects ex-offenders' post-release employment opportunities. Both the original study in Milwaukee and an expanded version of the same design in New York City produced nearly identical findings: A criminal record is a significant barrier to employment. Potential employers scrutinize black applicants more critically than white applicants. Indeed, a black applicant with no criminal record fares about the same as a white applicant with a criminal record. While a criminal record is indeed a significant barrier to employment, the stigma of race poses an equally large barrier.

➤ Read "Investigating Prisoner Reentry: The Impact of Conviction Status on the Employment Prospects of Young Men" by Devah Pager and Bruce Western at http://www.ncjrs.gov/pdffiles1/nij/grants/228584.pdf.

Evaluations of Hawaii HOPE

Two evaluations of Hawaii's innovative HOPE (Hawaii's Opportunity Probation with Enforcement) program found that participating probationers were significantly less likely to fail drug tests or miss probation appointments. They were also sentenced to less time in prison because of probation revocations than were probationers who did not take part in the program.

HOPE uses a "swift and sure punishment" approach to discourage probation violations. Judges give probationers "warning hearings" to tell them that probation terms will be strictly enforced. Frequent, unannounced drug testing is part of the program. Participants must call a hotline each weekday morning to learn if they will be drug-tested that day. A participant who fails a morning drug test is arrested immediately. They may be in court within a few hours, where the judge will change the terms of their probation to include a short stay in jail. Employed probationers are often allowed to serve their jail time on weekends, at least initially, to encourage continued employment.

The court also assures those who need drug treatment or mental health counseling that they will get the treatment they need, but that they are expected to attend and complete such programs. In the past, probationers might skip appointments with probation officers, fail many drug tests, or even drop out of treatment programs. Before HOPE, the consequences of these violations, such as probation revocation and a lengthy prison sentence, were typically delayed and uncertain. The HOPE approach is to respond immediately to probation violations, stressing swiftness and certainty, rather than severity.

Using a quasi-experimental design, researchers compared probationers who took part in the HOPE program with those who did not. HOPE probationers had large decreases in positive drug tests and missed appointments. They were much less likely to be arrested. They spent about the same number of days in jail for probation violations as the comparison group, serving more frequent but shorter terms. However, they were sentenced to about one-third as many days in prison as the non-HOPE group for probation revocations or new convictions. A one-year randomized control trial confirmed these results.

During the first three months after HOPE probationers started participating, they showed striking improvement in their drug use as positive drug tests fell from 53 percent to 9 percent. By contrast, positive drug tests for the non-HOPE group increased initially but showed negligible change over time. Results from the smaller but more rigorous one-year randomized control trial showed similar declines in problem outcomes among probationers in the HOPE treatment group.

➤ Visit http://www.nij.gov/topics/corrections/community/drug-offenders/hawaii-hope.htm.

CHAPTER 2:
TRANSLATING KNOWLEDGE TO PRACTICE

Elder Abuse

NIJ's research program focuses on the issue of elder mistreatment to help the field in its response to the current and emerging needs of the elderly population. Current studies are exploring several areas of elder forensics, assessing and identifying elder abuse in the field, and describing the nature of crimes against the elderly.

NIJ has released an annual, competitive research solicitation on the topic of elder abuse since 2005. The Institute held a workshop to refine the federal research agenda on elder abuse and neglect in February 2008. Researchers are developing and testing screening tools to help staff of Adult Protective Services and medical examiners more readily identify elder mistreatment. The Institute is also sponsoring an evaluation of an elder abuse forensics center.

NIJ funded research on measuring pressure ulcers (bedsores) as a possible forensic marker to identify neglect of the elderly. This work builds on previous research on bruising in the elderly, which helps professionals to distinguish between accidental bruising and abusive bruising. NIJ also sponsored research on detecting elder abuse in residential care centers and the extent of financial exploitation of the elderly. NIJ research makes it easier for professionals to detect elder abuse and provides law enforcement and prosecutors with a solid forensic basis for handling cases.

> ➢ Visit http://www.nij.gov/nij/topics/crime/elderabuse/welcome.htm.

Harvard Executive Session

NIJ and Harvard's Kennedy School of Government are collaborating on an Executive Session on Policing and Public Safety, which brings together leading police executives and scholars. The Executive Session supports continuing inquiry, analysis and communication between researchers and the law enforcement community. The sessions allow participants to challenge conventional wisdom about the nature of problems and the policies and strategies needed to solve them. Together, the members of the Executive Session will elaborate the strategies and frameworks needed for policing. Although setting a research agenda is not the primary purpose of the Executive Session, research ideas will likely emerge from several working papers that are being published over the course of the project period.

> ➤ Learn more about the Harvard Executive Sessions on Policing and Public Safety and read all of the papers published so far at http://www.nij.gov/topics/law-enforcement/administration/executive-sessions/welcome.htm.

Predictive Policing Symposia

NIJ and the Bureau of Justice Assistance sponsored symposia on predictive policing with the Los Angeles Police Department, the Providence Police Department and Roger Williams University. These forums brought together researchers, practitioners and criminal justice leaders to discuss the idea of predictive policing and its impact on crime and justice.

Predictive policing involves gathering crime information from various sources, analyzing it and then using the results to anticipate, prevent and respond more effectively to future crime. These were the first national discussions of this topic. Participants shared current knowledge about predictive policing, presented case studies and addressed developments. The Los Angeles meeting focused mainly on large police departments, while the Providence meeting was geared toward the needs of smaller and rural departments.

Meanwhile, NIJ has launched a pilot project to develop, test and evaluate predictive policing in a real-world, real-time context. The Institute awarded planning grants to seven law enforcement agencies. Of the seven, a smaller number of sites will be selected to participate in a demonstration program. NIJ has also funded a team from the RAND Corp. to evaluate the projects.

> ➤ Read "Predictive Policing: The Future of Law Enforcement?" by Beth Pearsall in NIJ Journal no.266 at http://www.nij.gov/journals/266/predictive.htm.

Forensic Science Training and Cold Case Funding

When an envelope full of an unidentified white powder turns up in an office, how should forensic scientists proceed? What is the best way to handle evidence collection at a clandestine grave that may contain more than one body? NIJ training programs cover everything from crime scene investigations to sophisticated DNA analysis techniques. Many training sessions are held at various locations around the country, while others are available online. All training sessions are free to state and local forensic science practitioners, law enforcement professionals and criminal justice partners.

NIJ has also funded a series of cold case trainings through the Virginia Center for Policing Innovation to help solve cold cases by using DNA evidence. As a result, police departments have solved some serious crime cases, sometimes bringing people to justice decades after the crime was committed. In fiscal year 2009, NIJ awarded about $12 million in cold case funding to state and local law enforcement agencies. In one dramatic case this year, detectives in Grand Rapids, Mich., arrested a man in the murder of Diane Holloway, a 21-year-old who had been killed in 1979. In a similar case, Los Angeles detectives were able to make an arrest in the murder of 33-year-old Sandra Faith Phillips, who had been killed in 1979.

> ➢ For information about NIJ training courses, visit http://www.nij.gov/training/ all-courses.htm.

CHAPTER 3:
ADVANCING TECHNOLOGY

DNA Testing Backlog

In 2004, in response to the emerging DNA testing backlog, Congress passed legislation to fund programs that would reduce the backlog and improve the use of DNA technology in the criminal justice system. The legislation had several objectives, among them to reduce the backlog and build up the nation's database of DNA profiles. By 2010, hundreds of millions of dollars had been spent to achieve these goals. Data confirm that federal funding has had a significant impact on the backlog. Without the influx of federal support between 2005 and 2008, the backlog problem would be much worse.

In June 2010, NIJ published *Making Sense of DNA Backlogs – Myths vs. Reality*, an analysis of progress on DNA testing from 2005 to 2008. According to grant reports sent to NIJ and surveys of crime labs, NIJ's DNA Backlog Reduction Program has helped fund crime laboratories nationwide to reduce backlogs by 135,753 cases. State and local DNA laboratories increased their capacity to work cases by almost threefold between 2005 and 2008. Without the federal funds to buy better equipment and hire more personnel, many laboratories would not have been able to increase their capacity much beyond the reported 2005 levels. While older cases have been processed, the increasing demand for DNA processing has outstripped the capacity of the nation's crime laboratories.

NIJ's largest funding program is the DNA Backlog Reduction Program, which has provided $330 million in direct grants to accredited public-sector DNA laboratories between 2004 and 2009.

The program's short-term goal is to reduce the backlog of untested cases by providing crime laboratories with funds to work more cases. The crime laboratories can send backlogged cases to private laboratories or test more cases in-house.

The long-term goal is to build the capacity of crime laboratories. Labs use the funds to buy high-throughput instruments that can handle multiple samples simultaneously, automated robotic systems and information management systems to process the data produced more efficiently and confirm newer, more efficient laboratory procedures. Funds also can be used to hire more personnel.

> ➤ See "Making Sense of DNA Backlogs –
>   Myths vs. Reality" by Mark Nelson at
>   http://www.ncjrs.gov/pdffiles1/nij/
>   230183.pdf.
> ➤ Visit http://www.dna.gov/funding/
>   dna-backlog-reduction.

Postconviction DNA

More than 250 Americans convicted of serious crimes have been freed from prison after DNA testing showed they could not have committed the crimes of which they were accused. DNA testing has improved a great deal in recent years, and new testing techniques can yield definitive results in cases that may have been inconclusive in the past. In many of the exoneration cases, DNA testing was not available when the people were convicted.

NIJ's Postconviction Testing Assistance Program helps states pay for reviewing cases of murder, manslaughter and rape, including finding and analyzing the evidence that can prove innocence. The funding provides money to increase the number of cases reviewed. The states that receive the awards agree to comply with improved standards for storing biological evidence. In 2010, NIJ awarded a total of $1.56 million to Illinois, Maryland, Minnesota and Washington. NIJ currently funds DNA testing in 14 states.

> ➤ Visit http://www.dna.gov/funding/
>   postconviction.

New Forensics Tool to Detect Hidden Graves

Sometimes law enforcement officials get a tip about a hidden grave, but the information they receive may be vague, simply indicating a general area where something may be found. A search may involve many people attempting to cover a large area.

NIJ has funded development of a new tool for detecting hidden graves. Scientists at Oak Ridge National Laboratory and the University of Tennessee developed the tool. Using a specific and unique database of human decomposition odors, this project developed a sensor package that can find clandestine graves. The detector was built with off-the-shelf parts and is designed to detect the major classes of chemical compounds relevant in human decomposition. It is self-contained, portable and built for field use. The detector provides both visual and auditory cues to the operator. The detector is called the LABRADOR, an acronym for "lightweight analyzer for buried remains and decomposition odor recognition." The detector's batteries, if fully charged, will last up to six hours of constant use. The cost is about $1,000-$1,500 for each unit. The database composing the odor emanation from human cadavers was developed at Oak Ridge National Laboratory with the University of Tennessee's Anthropological Research Facility, and it continues to be developed for long-term burials. The research team also developed an accompanying computer program for the device, which is available to forensic teams.

> Read "A New Forensics Tool: Development of an Advanced Sensor for Detecting Clandestine Graves" by Arpad Vass, Cyril V. Thompson and Marc Wise at http://www.ncjrs.gov/pdffiles1/ nij/grants/231197.pdf.

Communications Technology

The Institute continued work on communications technology for law enforcement and corrections. For example, NIJ, the Federal Communications Commission and the Federal Bureau of Prisons are developing a plan to address the issue of illegal cell phone use by offenders in jails and prisons. NIJ also is working closely with the National Telecommunications and Information Administration to develop the public safety part of the National Broadband Plan.

Meanwhile, NIJ is sponsoring development of advanced radio technology for law enforcement agencies. For example, one project involves developing cognitive radio protocols and platforms for dynamic spectrum access in public

safety networks. This would allow agencies to communicate on different wireless networks simultaneously. The bonding of networks would also allow video streaming and other features that may not be supported on any single radio network because of bandwidth constraints.

> For a brief report on the problem of cell phones behind bars, see http://www.ncjrs.gov/pdffiles1/nij/ 227539.pdf.

Hazardous Materials Standard

In fiscal year 2010, NIJ made final modifications to its draft standard for equipment to protect law enforcement officers responding to situations involving chemical, biological, radiological and nuclear (CBRN) hazards. This was one of the law enforcement community's highest priority technology needs. This program caps several years of development of collaborative partnerships with the Department of Homeland Security, the U.S. Army Natick Soldier Research, Development and Engineering Center, police organizations and the National Fire Protection Association. All of these organizations now support NIJ's work on the standard for an ensemble worn by police who respond to CBRN events, including toxic spills and methamphetamine labs. NIJ published the standard in November 2010.

> See http://www.ncjrs.gov/pdffiles1/nij/ 221916.pdf

The National Missing and Unidentified Persons System (NamUs)

NamUs was developed in response to an overwhelming need for a centralized reporting system for unidentified human remains cases and missing person cases. NIJ collaborated with medical examiners and coroners, law enforcement agencies, advocacy groups and the public, including families of those lost. The result of this collaboration is the computerized NamUs system, which anyone can use to search records of missing persons and unidentified persons cases. In the past, these records were not easily accessed. In addition, the public was unable to search the available information or to help in these cases because existing databases were restricted to law enforcement access. Historically, families looking for loved ones had to call many agencies and look to several websites to find the information that now exists in one place. The recent development and launch of the NamUs web site for NIJ is a groundbreaking step toward faster resolution of missing persons and unidentified persons cases, benefiting law enforcement and the community as a whole.

On September 30, 2010, there were 11,732 open cases in NamUs, and these numbers continue to increase every day. At the time of publication, NamUs had helped to resolve 18 unidentified persons cases and 35 missing persons cases.

> ➢ See www.namus.gov.

CHAPTER 4:
WORKING ACROSS DISCIPLINES

Officer Safety on the Roads

NIJ has collaborated with fire service and automotive engineering agencies on several studies to keep officers safe on the side of roads. Increasing the visibility of emergency vehicles and developing training and tools aimed at keeping first responders safe on the road have emerged as next steps in the effort to prevent officer deaths.

A recent study took a closer look at some commercially available products to see whether they help increase emergency vehicle visibility and improve roadway safety for both emergency responders and the public. The study was funded by NIJ and conducted by the U.S. Fire Administration (USFA) and the International Fire Service Training Association. They found, among other things, that retro-reflective materials can help heighten emergency vehicle visibility, especially during nighttime conditions, and that using contrasting colors can help civilian drivers find a hazard amid the visual clutter of the roadway. NIJ is also collaborating with the USFA on a website that has the latest information and research about roadside safety for first responders.

> ➤ See http://www.respondersafety.com.

Preliminary data for 2009 from the National Law Enforcement Officers Memorial Fund show that for the twelfth year in a row, more officers were killed in traffic incidents than from any other cause of death, including shootings. By October 2009, 48 law enforcement officers had died in traffic-related incidents, accounting for close to 50 percent of officer deaths for the year.

➢ Read "Keeping Officers Safe on the Road" by Beth Pearsall in NIJ Journal no. 265 at http://www.nij.gov/journals/ 265/officers.htm.

Survey of Unanalyzed Law Enforcement Evidence

The large backlog of evidence awaiting analysis in the nation's crime labs has received much attention of late. A recent NIJ-funded survey looked at a related issue — forensic evidence stored in police property rooms that has not gone to a lab for analysis. The survey included more than 2,000 police departments. Researchers determined that forensic evidence existed but had not been sent to a lab in 14 percent of open homicide cases, 18 percent of open rape cases and 23 percent of open property crime cases.

The findings suggest that some law enforcement agencies may not fully understand the potential value of forensic evidence in developing new leads in a criminal investigation. Reasons cited by police departments for not sending evidence to labs were: the suspect had not been identified (in 44 percent of the cases), the suspect was adjudicated (in 24 percent of cases), the case was dismissed, the officers did not feel the analysis was needed, the suspect was not charged, or analysis was not requested by a prosecutor. In six percent of cases, the police department reported not sending the evidence to the lab because they believed the laboratory would not accept forensic evidence due to their backlog. The survey helped criminal

justice practitioners to get a better picture of how evidence is handled and why it is sometimes not processed at all.

➢ Read "Untested Evidence: Not Just a Crime Lab Issue" by NIJ Communications Staff in NIJ Journal no. 266 at http://www.nij.gov/journals/266/ untested.htm.

Electronic Monitoring

A large NIJ-funded study of Florida offenders placed on electronic monitoring found that monitoring significantly reduces the likelihood of failure under community supervision. The decline in the risk of failure is about 31 percent overall, compared to offenders placed on other forms of community supervision. Electronic monitoring reduced the failure rate by 26 percent for violent offenders and by 36 percent for sex, property, drug and other offenders.

Researchers from Florida State University's Center for Criminology and Public Policy Research compared the experiences of more than 5,000 medium- and high-risk offenders who were monitored electronically to more than 266,000 offenders not placed on monitoring over a six-year period. The researchers worked with the Florida Department of Corrections to secure approval, get administrative data and get help to contact local probation offices for interviews. The researchers interviewed offenders, probation officers, supervisors and administrators to gain more insights into electronic monitoring.

States now employ electronic monitoring in a wide variety of settings, such as a pretrial supervision alternative to jail, an alternative to imprisonment for some offenders, and a mandated supervision requirement for some felons released from prison. Some states now mandate electronic monitoring for released sex offenders. More than 5.1 million offenders in the United States are under some form of community supervision, and electronic monitoring may increase over time as states seek less expensive alternatives to imprisonment. The cost of imprisonment is about six times higher than the cost of electronic monitoring.

> ➤ Read "A Quantitative and Qualitative Assessment of Electronic Monitoring" by William Bales, Karen Mann, Thomas Blomberg, Gerry Gaes, Kelle Barrick, Karla Dhungana and Brian McManus at http://www.ncjrs.gov/pdffiles1/nij/grants/230530.pdf.

CHAPTER 5:
ADOPTING A GLOBAL PERSPECTIVE

NIJ's International Center

NIJ's International Center provides a global perspective for criminal justice practitioners and researchers.

The Center published several reports on developments in overseas criminal justice systems that highlight innovative programs that could be adopted in the United States. These transferability assessments include information about how the programs work and what their strengths and weaknesses are. Topics have included day fines, an alternative to prison that is used in Europe and Latin America, and virtual autopsies, which use advanced imaging equipment to help determine a cause of death.

The Center has reinvigorated research on international organized crime. In January 2010, NIJ hosted more than 50 experts and practitioners from around the globe to explore the state of knowledge in this area. The Center also published a research solicitation on international organized crime and selected two projects for funding. NIJ's efforts in international organized crime research are coordinated with other federal agencies and law enforcement agencies in the United Kingdom, Canada, Australia and Germany.

The Center sponsored international workshops on human trafficking, transnational organized crime and wrongful convictions.

Also, the Center routinely hosts foreign professionals who are visiting the United States to learn more about the American criminal justice system. In fiscal year 2010, the Center had 102 visitors from 45 countries.

APPENDIX: FINANCIAL DATA

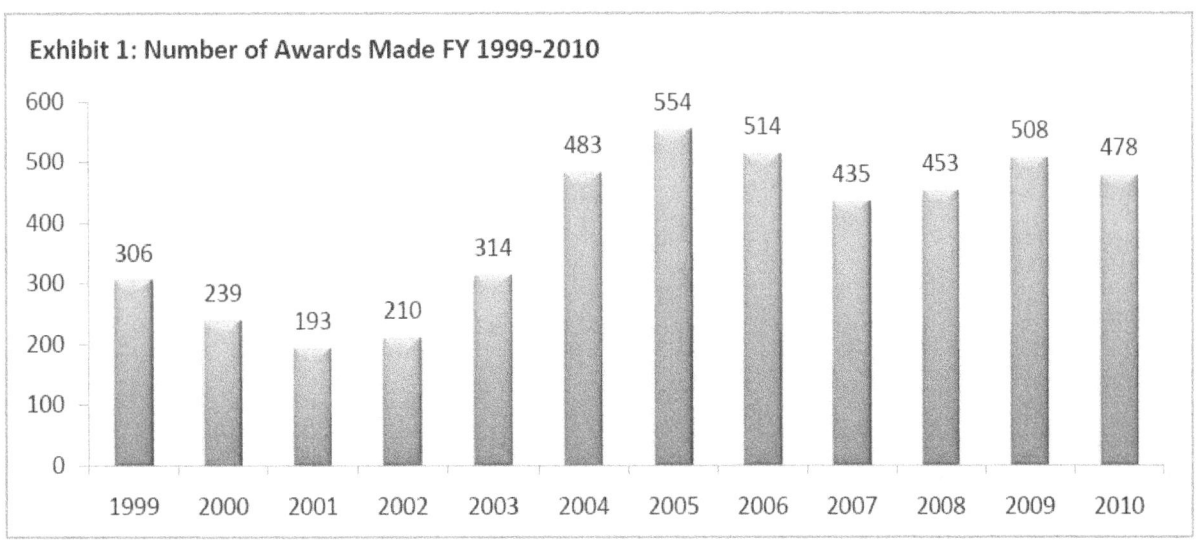

Exhibit 1: Number of Awards Made FY 1999-2010

Year	Number of Awards
1999	306
2000	239
2001	193
2002	210
2003	314
2004	483
2005	554
2006	514
2007	435
2008	453
2009	508
2010	478

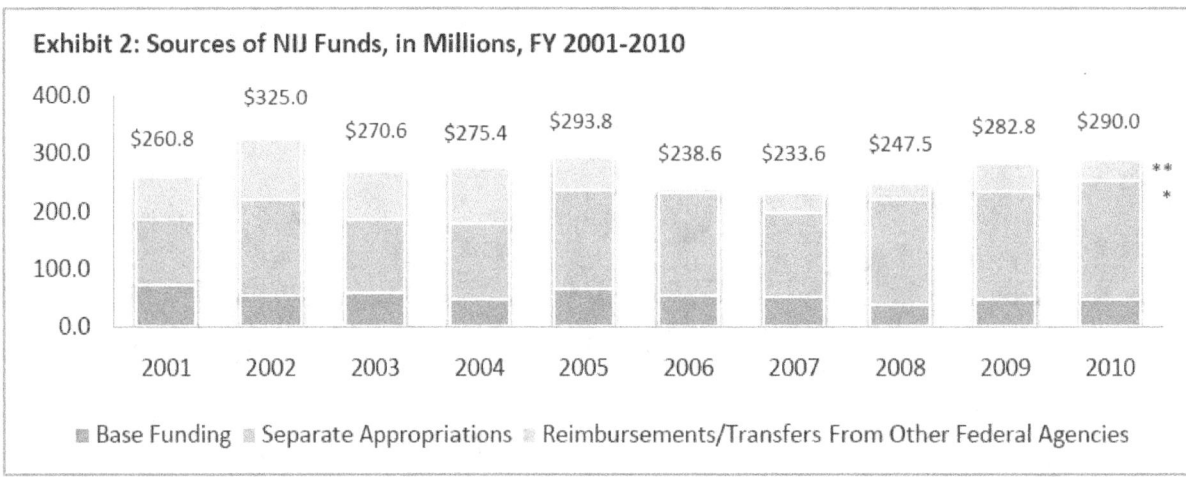

Exhibit 2: Sources of NIJ Funds, in Millions, FY 2001-2010

*In 2010, separate appropriations includes funds appropriated by Public Law 111-117 as follows: (1) under the Community Oriented Policing Services heading, $161 million for DNA related and forensic programs and activities; (2) under the State and Local Law Enforcement Assistance heading, $35 million for Paul Coverdell Forensic Science Improvement Grants, $1 million for analysis and research on violence against Indian women, and $5 million for use in assisting units of local government to identify, select, develop, modernize and purchase new technologies for use by law enforcement; and (3) under the Violence Against Women heading, $3 million for research and evaluation of violence against women and related issues.

**In 2010, reimbursements/transfers from other federal agencies include the following: (1) $7 million made available to NIJ pursuant to Section 215 of Public Law 111-117 (Assistant Attorney General set-aside authority); (2) $10 million for prisoner reentry research from the offender reentry programs ("Second Chance Act") appropriation administered by OJP's BJA; (3) $1.5 million for related research, testing, and evaluation programs from the appropriation for the Bulletproof Vest Partnership program administered by BJA; and (4) $18.7 million for various projects funded by other Federal entities, including other OJP components.

Exhibit 3: Allocation of NIJ Funds as a Percentage of Total Funding, FY 2010*

Social Science	Evaluation	3.4%
	Research	7.8%
Science and Technology	Research and Development	3.9%
	Standards Development	1.2%
	Technology Assistance/ Test and Evaluation	7.9%
	Training	0.4%
Investigative and Forensic Science	Analysis and Capacity Enhancement**	46.0%
	Research and Development	11.4%
	Technology Assistance/ Test and Evaluation	2.3%
	Training	3.6%
	National Missing and Unidentified Persons System (NamUs)	0.9%
Dissemination/Outreach		2.1%
Program Support		3.9%
Reprogrammed per Congressional Notice to Salaries and Expenses		1.7%
Carryover***		3.5%

*Sources of NIJ total funding of $290 million are shown in Exhibit 2.

**Grants to improve and enhance crime laboratories (including funds for analyses/backlog reduction).

***NIJ received funding for these programs in FY 2010 (funds that do not expire at the end of the fiscal year). "Carryover" funds are those that remained unobligated as of the end of the fiscal year. Depending on the provisions of future appropriations legislation, these funds may be subject to statutory rescission.

Exhibit 4: Funding for DNA Related Forensic Programs and Activities, FY 2010

The National Institute of Justice received $161 million in FY 2010 appropriations for DNA related to forensic programs and activities, which were used as follows:

DNA Analysis and Capacity Enhancement and for Other Forensic Activities	in millions
Forensic DNA Backlog Reduction	$64.80
Convicted Offender and/or Arrestee DNA Backlog Reduction	$4.60
Solving Cold Cases with DNA	$10.10
Forensic DNA Unit Efficiency	$0.20
Using DNA to Identify the Missing	$5.40
Forensic Science Training Development and Delivery	$8.00
Research, Development and Evaluation	$26.50
Forensic Technology Center of Excellence	$6.20
Strategic Approaches to Sexual Assault Kit (SAK) Evidence: An Action Research Project*	$1.00
Related Activities, including National Missing and Unidentified Persons System (NamUs); conferences and scientific and technical working group meetings; final product reviews; and dissemination/publication of DNA- and forensics-related products.	$17.80
Reprogrammed per Congressional Notice for Salaries and Expenses	$2.30
Carryover**	$4.10
SUBTOTAL	$151.00

Postconviction DNA Testing Assistance	in millions
Postconviction DNA Testing Assistance Program Grants	$1.60
Related Activities	$0.30
Reprogrammed per Congressional Notice for Salaries and Expenses	$0.10
Carryover**	$3.00
SUBTOTAL	$5.00

Sexual Assault Forensic Exam Program	in millions
Development, Delivery, and Evaluation of Sexual Assault Forensic Training Programs	$2.40
Reprogramming per Congressional Notice for Salaries and Expenses	$0.10
Carryover**	$2.50
SUBTOTAL	$5.00
TOTAL	$161.00

* Grants were awarded in FY 2011 with FY 2010 funds.

**NIJ receives "no-year" funding for these programs (funds that do not expire at the end of the fiscal year). "Carryover" funds are those that remained unobligated as of the end of the fiscal year. Depending on the provisions of future appropriations legislation, these funds may be subject to statutory rescission.

Exhibit 5: The Nature of BJA-Funded Evaluation Research and Development Activities under the Byrne Formula and Discretionary Grant Programs 2010

The National Institute of Justice received $5 million from Edward Byrne Memorial Justice Assistance Grant program to help local governments identify, select, develop, modernize and purchase new technologies for use by law enforcement.

	in millions
Research on Policing Technology	$0.05
Officer Safety Technology Research and Development	$0.59
Crime Mapping and Geospatial Tool Research and Development	$0.77
Corrections Technology Demonstration and Evaluation	$0.30
Offender Tracking Technology Research	$0.77
Training Technology Research and Development	$0.53
Improved Information Delivery to the Officer at the Scene Research and Development	$0.47
Equipment Compliance Testing	$1.38
Body Armor Research and Development	$0.03
Program Support and Other Administrative Rescissions	$0.10
TOTAL	$5.00